Phonograph to Streaming Music

Then to Now Tech

By Jennifer Colby

21st Century **Junior** Library

Published in the United States of America by
Cherry Lake Publishing
Ann Arbor, Michigan
www.cherrylakepublishing.com

Content Adviser: Adam Fulton Johnson, PhD History of Science and Technology, University of Michigan
Reading Adviser: Marla Conn, MS, Ed., Literacy specialist, Read-Ability, Inc.

Photo Credits: ©jakkapan/Shutterstock.com, Cover, 1 [left]; ©Africa Studio/Shutterstock.com, Cover, 2 [right]; Library of Congress, LC-USZ62-98128, 4; ©Everett Historical/Shutterstock.com, 6; ©Terence Mendoza/Shutterstock.com, 8; ©VK Studio/Shutterstock.com, 10; ©I love photo/Shutterstock.com, 12; ©JOKE777/Shutterstock.com, 14; ©Heidi Schneider/Shutterstock.com, 16; ©Ralph Gillen/Shutterstock.com, 18; ©Arthurstock/Shutterstock.com, 20

Library of Congress Cataloging-in-Publication Data
Names: Colby, Jennifer, 1971- author.
Title: Phonograph to streaming music / Jennifer Colby.
Description: Ann Arbor : Cherry Lake Publishing, 2019. | Series: Then to now tech | Includes bibliographical references and index. | Audience: K to grade 3.
Identifiers: LCCN 2019004225| ISBN 9781534147270 (hardcover) | ISBN 9781534148703 (pdf) | ISBN 9781534150133 (pbk.) | ISBN 9781534151567 (hosted ebook)
Subjects: LCSH: Sound–Recording and reproducing–History–Juvenile literature.
Classification: LCC TK7881.4 .C647 2019 | DDC 621.389/309–dc23
LC record available at https://lccn.loc.gov/2019004225

Cherry Lake Publishing would like to acknowledge the work of the Partnership for 21st Century Skills. Please visit *www.p21.org* for more information.

Printed in the United States of America
Corporate Graphics

CONTENTS

The first words Edison recorded on his device were "Mary had a little lamb."

First Recorded Words

Thomas Edison invented many things. While working on the **telegraph** and the telephone in 1877, he figured out a way to **record** and play sound. This device was called the **phonograph**.

People would fill concert halls to hear phonographs played.

Music at Your Fingertips

Before the phonograph, there was only one way to listen to music: live. You had to either be there when someone was playing an instrument, or play the instrument yourself. Edison's phonograph allowed people to hear music anytime they wanted. Soldiers fighting in World War I enjoyed music from specially made Edison phonographs.

The harder wax cylinders could be played over 100 times!

At first, recordings were made on wax **cylinders**. But they were difficult to create. And sound quality became poor after only a few dozen playings. New developments resulted in harder wax cylinders that could be copied more easily.

Make a Guess!

Wax cylinders had a limited recording time. Guess how many minutes of music could be recorded on a cylinder.

With the transition of wax cylinders to discs, the new versions of phonographs were called gramophones.

Listening on the Go

By 1912, the **disc record** became more popular than wax cylinders for recording and playing music. These records were played on a **record player**. Easier to produce, they could hold about 3 minutes of music on each side. The long-playing record, also called the **album**, was introduced in the 1940s. It could hold more than three times the amount of music on each side.

Radios like this could be taken anywhere.

Despite their popularity, record players were not very **portable**. And radio stations, broadcasting free music, were popping up around the world. By the late 1950s, small and simple **transistor radios** allowed people to listen to music anywhere.

Look!

Today we use many different devices to play music. Look around your house. What types of devices does your family use to play music?

Sony's Walkman was a fun new way to listen to music on the go.

The **invention** of the audio **cassette tape** in 1963 allowed people to make their own mixtapes. They could create collections of their favorite music and share them with others.

In 1979, Sony introduced the Walkman, a portable cassette player with headphones for personal listening. It **evolved** into a portable disc player in 1984 with the development of **compact discs** (CDs).

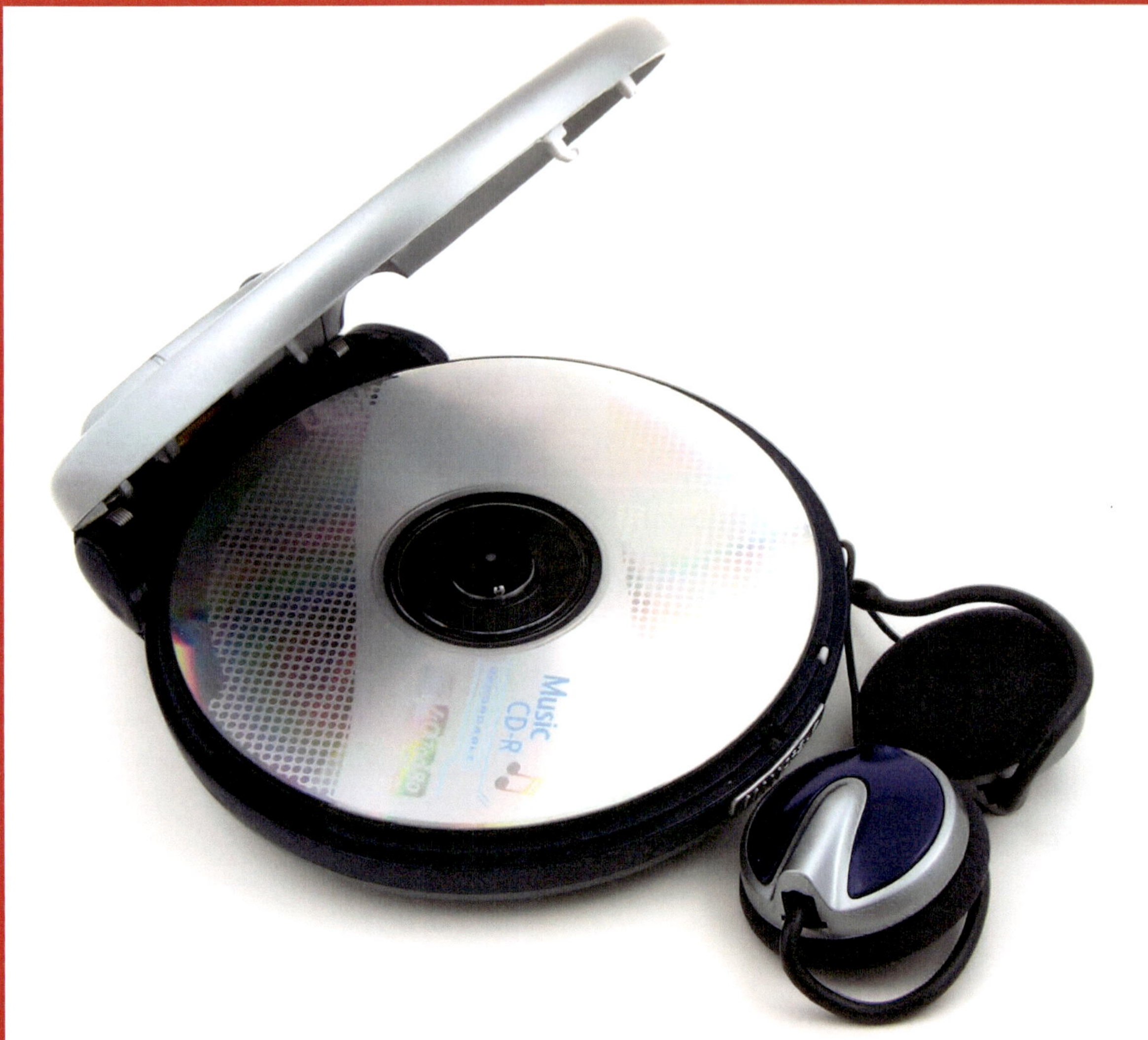

Before music streaming services, CD players were all the rage in the 1990s.

Music Online

With the development of the internet came more access to **digital music**. Before then, if you wanted to own a recording from your favorite band, you had to go to a record store to buy it.

The iPhone has taken over iPod sales. The iPod classic was discontinued in 2014.

More access to digital music led to the development of devices to play it. Many companies began producing these devices. Apple's iPod was the most popular for many years. Released in 2001, it could store and play 1,000 songs.

Think!

Where does your family get music from? Maybe your parents still play music from compact discs or records. Or maybe they use streaming services. What do you think is better?

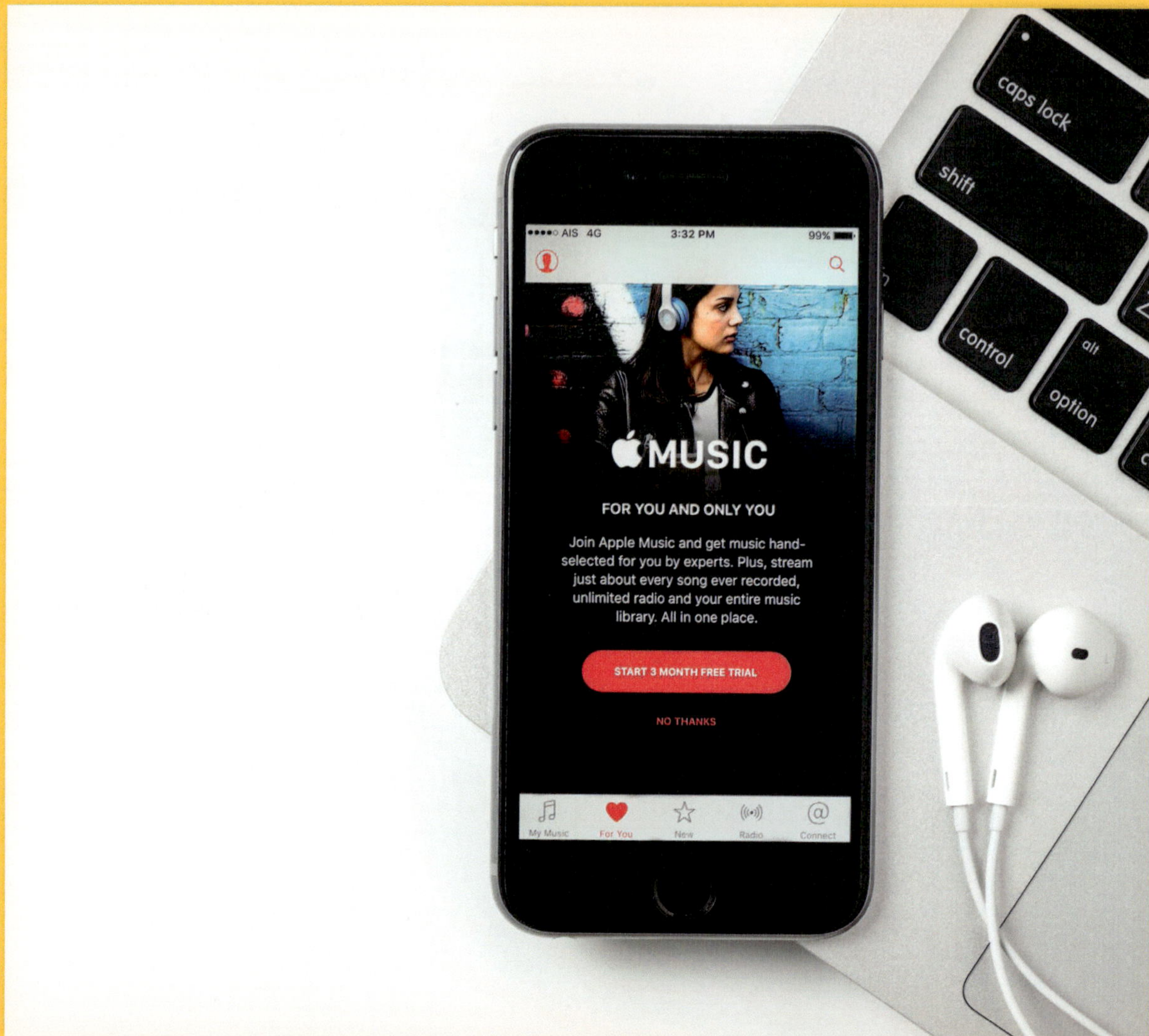

There are many music streaming services.

Popularized in the 2010s, music streaming services allow people to play music directly from the internet. Popular streaming services include Apple Music, Spotify, and Pandora.

Though the methods for listening to music have changed over the years, our love of listening to music has not.

Ask Questions!

Do you have a favorite music streaming service? What about your friends or family? Take a survey to find out which service is the most popular.

GLOSSARY

album (AL-buhm) a long musical recording on a record or CD that usually includes a set of songs

cassette tape (kuh-SET TAYP) a case containing a length of magnetic tape that runs between two small reels, used for recording or playback of audio

compact discs (KOM-pakt DISKS) a small, flat, round piece of plastic on which music is recorded

cylinders (SIL-uhn-durz) objects with flat, circular ends and sides shaped like the outside of a tube

digital music (DIJ-ih-tuhl MYOO-zik) music that has been recorded in or converted to a file that a computer can read and play

disc record (DISK REK-urd) a flat, round, circular object with grooves on which music can be recorded and played

evolved (ih-VOLVD) changed over time into a more advanced state

invention (in-VEN-shun) something new and useful

phonograph (FOH-nuh-graf) an early sound recording and playing device

portable (POR-tuh-buhl) easy to carry around

record (rih-KORD) to store sounds and music so that they can be heard later

record player (REK-urd PLAY-ur) a more modern machine that plays recordings of music

telegraph (TEL-ih-graf) an early system of sending messages over long distances by using wires and electrical signals

transistor radios (tran-ZIS-ter RAY-dee-ohz) small, battery-operated radio receivers

FIND OUT MORE

BOOKS

Boone, Mary. *Thomas Edison*. North Mankato, MN: Capstone Press, 2018.

Burgan, Michael. *Spotify, Pandora, and Streaming Music*. Broomall, PA: Mason Crest Publishers, 2018.

WEBSITES

ThoughtCo.—Edison's Invention of the Phonograph
https://www.thoughtco.com/invention-of-the-phonograph-4156528
Learn more about Thomas Edison's favorite invention.

Wonderopolis—How Do You Listen to Music?
https://wonderopolis.org/wonder/how-do-you-listen-to-music
Learn more about how the way we listen to music has changed over the years.

INDEX

ABOUT THE AUTHOR

Jennifer Colby is a school librarian in Ann Arbor, Michigan. She loves reading, traveling, and going to museums to learn about new things.